T0347452

DIRTY HARE PRODUCTIONS PRESENTS

Gunter

Co-created by Lydia Higman, Julia Grogan & Rachel Lemon

Gunter was first performed at Summerhall on Wednesday 2 August 2023 and at the Royal Court Jerwood Theatre Upstairs, Sloane Square, on Wednesday 3 April 2024.

Gunter
Co-created by Lydia Higman, Julia Grogan & Rachel Lemon

Cast (in alphabetical order)

Julia Grogan
Lydia Higman
Hannah Jarrett-Scott
Norah Lopez Holden

Director **Rachel Lemon**
Designer **Anna Orton**
Lighting Designer **Amy Daniels**
Composer & Lyricist, & Sound Designer **Lydia Higman**
Sound Designer **Tom Alford**
Associate Designer **Anisha Fields**
Movement Director & Choreographer **Aline David**
Video/Projection **Michelle Alise**
Voice Coach **Rebecca Whitbread**
Sound Design Consultant **Tom Foskett-Barnes**
Production Manager **Helen Mugridge**
Stage Manager **Aime Neeme**
Assistant Stage Manager **Molly Hands**

From the Royal Court, on this production:

Captioners **Jess Andrews & Rachel Dudley**
Stage Supervisor **Steve Evans & Maddy Collins**
Lead Producer **Hannah Lyall**
Sound Supervisors **David McSeveney & Jet Sharp**
Lighting Supervisors **Lucinda Plummer & Deanna Towli**
Costume Supervisors **Katie Price & Lucy Walshaw**
Company Manager **Mica Taylor**

The Royal Court Theatre and Stage Management wish to thank the following for their help with this production:
Sarah Georgeson, Chris James.

Lydia Higman (Co-creator, Cast, Composer & Lyricist, & Sound Designer)

Lydia Higman is a historian, writer and musician. She has a broad interest in the history of emotion, and how this area relates to sexuality and political thought. She has consulted on a range of theatre projects, history books, and co-wrote Belly Up with Julia. She is also the main songwriter for her all-female folk band, Iris & Steel, who recently played on the Alcove Stage at Latitude Festival.

Julia Grogan (Co-creator & Cast)

Julia trained as an actor at Rose Bruford College. She wrote her debut play Playfight while on the Royal Court Writers' Group. She has been a Writer on Attachment at the RSC and part of Channel 4 Screenwriters. She is currently developing original work with Hat Trick and she has her first feature film in development.

Theatre includes: **Belly Up (VAULT Festival/Turbine), Playfight (Theatre Uncut).**

Film includes: **Lives at Steak.**

Awards include: **The Experienced Theatre Practitioners Early Playwriting Award (Playfight); Samuel French Festival (Dogs of Society).**

Rachel Lemon (Co-creator & Director)

Rachel Lemon is a theatre director. She trained at Rose Bruford and on the National Theatre Directors course.

Theatre includes: **Bottom (Summerhall, Soho & UK Tour); Stripped! [co-director], Belly Up (Turbine).**

Amy Daniels (Lighting Designer)

Amy Daniels is a London-based lighting designer and technician working across theatre and live performance.

Theatre includes: **The Death & Life Of All Of Us (Victor Esses); A Suffocating Choking Feeling (TomYumSim); Antisemitism: (((a musical))) (Jessie Anand Productions); The Wetsuitman (Foreign Affairs); Declan (Alistair Hall); The Unicorn (NINA Productions); Rise (Kiln); There Was A Little Girl (Millie Wood-Downie); No Place Like Home (Alex Roberts &co); Dev's Army, The Matchbox, Quietly (Strange Fish).**

Anisha Fields (Associate Designer)

Anisha is a Set and Costume Designer, and graduate of the Bristol Old Vic Theatre School. She was resident at the RSC 2018-2019 and is an Associate Artist at Theatr Iolo.

As designer, theatre includes: **Pandemonium, Self-Raising (& Graeae) (Soho); Wendy: A Peter Pan Story, I Wish I Was A Mountain (& Travelling Light), Squirrel (& Unicorn) (Theatre Royal Bath); The Limit (ROH); Octopolis, Blackout Songs (Hampstead); Mom, How Did You Meet The Beatles? (Chichester Festival); Walworth Farce, Yellowfin (Southwark Playhouse); Blood Wedding, The Lower Depths (RCSSD); Owl at Home (Theatr Iolo); Alice in Wonderland (Mercury); Zoombird (Coventry Capital of Culture); Kes (Theatre by the Lake); Who's Afraid of Virginia Woolf (& Salisbury Playhouse), Beautiful Thing, A View From the Bridge, Macbeth (Tobacco Factory); First Encounters: Merchant of Venice (RSC).**

As associate designer, theatre includes: **Camp Siegfried (Old Vic); Acis and Galatea (Early Opera Company/Buxton International Festival); Everybody's Talking About Jamie (Sheffield Theatres).**

Awards include: **Leverhulme Arts Scholarship, Guardian's 12 theatre stars to watch.**

Hannah Jarrett-Scott (Cast)

Theatre includes: **Same Team - A Street Soccer Story (Traverse/Wonderfools); Alright Sunshine (Óran Mór); Underwood Lane, Pride and Prejudice* (*sort of) (& Criterion/West End/UK Tour), Cinderfella, The Taming of the Shrew (& Sherman) (Tron); The Wolves, Janis Joplin: Full Tilt (Royal Stratford East).**

Television includes: **Outlander, Two Doors Down, Float, Annika, Scot Squad, Trust Me, Short Stuff.**

Awards include: **Olivier Award for Best Comedy & Broadway World UK Award for Best Supporting Performer in a New Production of a Play. (Pride and Prejudice* (*sort of)).**

Hannah is a singer-songwriter currently releasing music with CLR theory.

Norah Lopez Holden (Cast)

Theatre includes: **Shed: Exploded View, The Almighty Sometimes, Our Town (Royal Exchange); The Flea (Yard); The Art of Illusion (Hampstead); Hamlet (Young Vic); Equus (Royal Stratford East); The Winter's Tale/ Eyam (Globe); Ghosts (HOME); Epic Love and Pop Songs (Pleasance).**

Norah was nominated for the Ian Charleson Award 2022 for Ophelia in Hamlet.

Radio includes: **Our Friends In The North, and various other productions for BBC Radio 4.**

Helen Mugridge
(Production Manager)

Helen is an experienced creative production manager.

Theatre includes: **untitled f*ck m*ss s**gon play (& Royal Exchange), Chasing Hares, Best of Enemies (Young Vic); 40/40 (Two Destination Language/UK tour); A Dead Body in Taos (Fuel/UK tour); Oh Mother (Rash Dash/UK tour); Cupids Revenge (New Arts Club/UK tour); FORGE (Transform Festival); RED, Likely Story (Wales Millennium Centre); Gaping Hole (Ovalhouse); Little Wimmin, Figs in Wigs (UK tour); Class, Scottee (Edinburgh, Canada and UK tour); Atomic 50 (Greenwich and Docklands International Festival); Idol, Jamal Gerald (Transform Festival and Theatre in the Mill Bradford); I'm a Phoenix, Bitch, Bryony Kimmings (Grand Hall, BAC and International dates); Fat Blokes (Edinburgh and UK tour); The Shape of the Pain (Chinaplate/BAC); Golem, 1927 (West End, The Space/BBC, UK and International tour).**

Aime Neeme
(Stage Manager - On Book)

Aime is an Australian stage manager and theatre maker.

For the Royal Court: **Bullring Techno Makeout Jamz (& Ellie Keel Productions).**

Other theatre includes: **An Interrogation (Ellie Keel Productions); Hungry, Black Love, May Queen, Really Big and Really Loud (Paines Plough); , How to Save the Planet When You're a Young Carer and Broke, Parakeet (Boundless).**

Anna Orton (Designer)

Anna Orton is a designer working across Theatre, Dance, Opera and Exhibition.

Theatre includes: **Messiah, Robin Hood Legend of the Forgotten Forest and King Lear (Bristol Old Vic); Blond Eckbert and Acis & Galatea (Hans Otto Theatre, Germany); Adults (Traverse); Kidnapped (National Theatre of Scotland); This is Memorial Device (Royal Lyceum, Edinburgh); The Tsar Has His Photo Taken, La Bohème (Scottish Opera); Peter Pan and Wendy, A Christmas Carol (Pitlochry).**

She was recipient of the OLD VIC 12 Designer Affiliation in 2019, an MGC Futures recipient in 2021 and was the first JMK runner up in 2023.

Rebecca Whitbread (Voice Coach)

Rebecca has been a voice coach since 2016 and is currently Voice Coordinator and one of the lead voice teachers at Rose Bruford College.

Rebecca has also worked as a community music teacher, working with various marginalised groups and continues to teach singing from her home studio. She is a musician and singer. She has also worked as a producer and director on music videos and is currently directing a short film.

THE ROYAL COURT THEATRE

The Royal Court Theatre is the writers' theatre. It is a leading force in world theatre for cultivating and supporting writers - undiscovered, emerging and established.

Since 1956, we have commissioned and produced hundreds of writers, from John Osborne to Mohamed-Zain Dada. Royal Court plays from every decade are now performed on stages and taught in classrooms and universities across the globe.

Through the writers, the Royal Court is at the forefront of creating restless, alert, provocative theatre about now. We open our doors to the unheard voices and free thinkers that, through their writing, change our way of seeing.

We strive to create an environment in which differing voices and opinions can co-exist. In current times, it is becoming increasingly difficult for writers to write what they want or need to write without fear, and we will do everything we can to rise above a narrowing of viewpoints.

Through all our work, we strive to inspire audiences and influence future writers with radical thinking and provocative discussion.

🐦 royalcourt 🔲 royalcourttheatre

Supported using public funding by
**ARTS COUNCIL
ENGLAND**

ROYAL COURT SUPPORTERS

Our incredible community of supporters makes it possible for us to achieve our mission of nurturing and platforming writers at every stage of their careers. Our supporters are part of our essential fabric – they help to give us the freedom to take bigger and bolder risks in our work, develop and empower new voices, and create world-class theatre that challenges and disrupts the theatre ecology.

To all our supporters, thank you. You help us to write the future.

PUBLIC FUNDING

Supported using public funding by
**ARTS COUNCIL
ENGLAND**

CHARITABLE PARTNERS

BackstageTrust

COCKAYNE

T. S. ELIOT FOUNDATION

JERWOOD
FOUNDATION

CORPORATE SPONSORS
Aqua Financial Ltd
Cadogan
Edwardian Hotels, London
Sustainable Wine Solutions

**SIS
TER**

CORPORATE MEMBERS
Bloomberg Philanthopies
Sloane Stanley

TRUSTS AND FOUNDATIONS
Maria Björnson Memorial Fund
Martin Bowley Charitable Trust
Chalk Cliff Trust
The Noël Coward Foundation
Cowley Charitable Foundation
The Davidson Play GC Bursary
The Lynne Gagliano Writer's Award
The Golden Bottle Trust
The Harold Hyam Wingate Foundation
John Lyon's Charity
Clare McIntyre's Bursary
Old Possum's Practical Trust
The Austin & Hope Pilkington Trust
Richard Radcliffe Charitable Trust
Rose Foundation
Royal Victoria Hall Foundation
The Thistle Trust
The Thompson Family Charitable Trust

Let's be friends. With benefits.

Our Friends and Good Friends are part of the fabric of the Royal Court. They help us to create world-class theatre, and in return they receive early access to our shows and a range of exclusive benefits.

Join today and become a part of our community.

Become a Friend (from £40 a year)

Benefits include:
- Priority Booking
- Advanced access to £15 Monday tickets
- 10% discount in our Bar & Kitchen (including Court in the Square) and Samuel French bookshop

Become a Good Friend (from £95 a year)

In addition to the Friend benefits, our Good Friends also receive:

- Five complimentary playtexts for Royal Court productions
- An invitation for two to step behind the scenes of the Royal Court Theatre at a special event

Our Good Friends' membership also includes a voluntary donation. This extra support goes directly towards supporting our work and future, both on and off stage.

To become a Friend or a Good Friend, or to find out more about the different ways in which you can get involved, visit our website: royalcourttheatre. com/support-us

The English Stage Company at the Royal Court Theatre is a registered charity (No. 231242)

GUNTER

Lydia Higman, Julia Grogan
and Rachel Lemon

A Preface about People, Process and the Past

Jules

Five years ago, I had a call from Lydia about Anne Gunter. She was finishing uni and had come across the story of a young girl feigning possession. It sounded heavy and hectic, and we'd just written the fiftieth draft of our play *Belly Up*, so – like a fool – I ran a mile when she suggested it would make a fantastic new project.

Fast forward to July 2022 and I'm sitting outside a Brighton pub in the harrowing wind, listening to Lyd and Rachel's wild plan of making Anne Gunter's story into a stage show and being asked if I want to come on board. This time, a bit loose from the Amstel, I hear what they're suggesting and am immediately swept up in their vision. A world of pin vomiting, football and levitation. I was absolutely in. Sick of waiting around for replies to emails and all the usual bollocks that comes with our under-funded industry, we nail down three things: we will make and produce the play ourselves, it'll have three actors, and a historian will frame the action.

To get under the skin of *Gunter*, we had to get to grips with the early seventeenth century. This was easy for our resident historian, but for me and old Rach, it meant Post-it notes and a shitload of research. The three of us descended on Wildcard Studios (a beautiful cheap space for artists, since closed down), where we took our sandwiches and spent days dragging story beats out of the limited archives and wrestling with how many Thomases appear in Anne's tale. After weeks of grappling, we finally had a very loose shape of a story; it had lots of gaps but we knew enough to apply to the Edinburgh Fringe. And when Summerhall accepted the show for August 2023, we very quickly had to actually make it.

With ticket money left over from *Belly Up*, we were able to pay two of the most wicked actors out there – Norah Lopez Holden and Letty Thomas – to come and R&D the project with us in Pelican House. Lyd kicked off proceedings with a history presentation and Rach ran improvisations and set up scenes where the three of us actors played with the characters. At this point I was Brian – which was hilarious because I'm five foot four and have the frame of a dormouse. We went from Pelican House to Cornwall, where we learnt Lydia's haunting music and swam in the sea and I wasn't playing Brian any more and everything was happy. It was incredible because the gaps in the story started getting filled. We felt closer to Anne, if that's not too yikes to say.

Then everything became a bit serious because we'd got the phenomenal Hannah Jarrett-Scott on board, and we were sat in Tottenham Quaker Meeting House with a banjo and three weeks to rehearse and make a show. And so began the messiest, wildest devising process, handled with absolute fearless freedom by Rachel Lemon – who deserves an Olivier for being the most exquisite rudder in all the chaos. Tottenham Quaker House is a space so tranquil you can't quite imagine Hannah, dressed as Brian, shredding Franz Ferdinand in a wig. Or the occasional AA group member accidentally strolling in on Norah vomiting pins. Or me, dressed as a bear, gyrating in maple syrup. It was a magical three weeks. We'd start and end the day in true Quaker style, standing up if we were moved to speak. Sharing our fears and hopes for the project, slagging off arts cuts for making theatre so fucking impossible. We played a lot of volleyball to keep connected as a team, because the truth is it was a really tough process in moments, and we had very little time.

Then we were off to Edinburgh! Only to get the date of our tech rehearsal wrong. A four-hour tech, now reduced to two. And with most of the team still in London, I had to play Anne and Brian and nineteen other parts (life made) while our legendary lighting designer Amy Daniels managed to programme the entire show. We had to cancel our first performance and we cried the whole first day at the festival. So, do not be fooled by the Fringe First and the *Financial Times* review. We did not get off to a cracking start. But we bloody managed it. And it was absolutely glorious. And I am forever in awe of you, Lydia and Rachel – thank you for your ferocity and for letting me in on the curious world of Anne Gunter.

One thing I've taken from this process: if you're making work you believe in, and you've got good friends around you, the rest doesn't matter. Because you're doing it. And making work is hard at the moment, it's not being made any easier. So, we've all just got to keep doing it and doing it. Until, hopefully, it gets a little easier.

Another thing we've learnt from making *Gunter* is the value of space. Space is expensive and hard to come by. We are aware of the privilege we had making *Gunter*. We had kind people open their doors to us and without that – having failed in our Arts Council bid – we wouldn't have been able to make the show. Making theatre is expensive and taking work to festivals like the Edinburgh Fringe just isn't feasible for a lot of companies. Yet it's really one of the only places that celebrates new artists and work. So, something is going very wrong. And we need to keep fighting for that to change.

We want to thank the following people for making our journey that bit easier:

Tom Forster at Summerhall for taking a punt on us.

Doug Higman for your patience with us and for making the most amazing poster and graphics.

Gillian Holden for making the most exquisite curtains.

Claire Henley for making an amazing swan mask.

Matt Byam Shaw for your support from the beginning.

Georgia Bruce, Lucy Webb, Willy Hudson, Sabir Khan, Daisy Jacobs, Sammy Glover, Kate Newman, Stella von Koskull, Sarah Farrell, Aris Sabetai, everyone who came into rehearsals and shared their thoughts on the chaos.

Miriam, Fergus and Erin at Storytelling PR.

Tom Alford for your love of unusual sound design and 'yes man' energy.

Micky at Summerhall, who mopped up feathers and maple syrup every night.

Meg and the Wildcard lot, Pelican House, Tottenham Quaker Meeting House and the Royal Court.

Patrick Ashe.

Xa Milne.

Josh and Faith.

Jim Sharpe, whose *Bewitchment of Anne Gunter* (1999) was foundational to this show, and Lydia's first interaction with the case. Sharpe was a greatly admired historian and communicator, and this show wouldn't have been possible without his ingenuity.

Rachel

This published text of our show looks very proper and neat and shiny, and I think it's important to preface it by talking about the mess of making *Gunter*. We often found ourselves totally lost, struggling to see anything clearly and we were unsure if we'd ever find a way through. In these seemingly impossible moments, I found myself clinging to hazy lessons from the back of my brain that I've picked up somewhere along the way: they offered us a way through the chaos. I hope that sharing some of these lessons might be useful.

1) Don't worry about answers; worry about creating the conditions in which good artists can work well.

This show is full of ideas that have been thought of, built upon, moulded and changed by all the artists who touched this production. There is a section named 'Anne's Performance' and every time we would get to it, Norah, playing Anne, would ask with dread: 'What are we going to do?' We didn't really know and it felt scary. Actually, by creating the conditions in which good work could happen, rather than trying to solve it on my own, we answered our own question. Invite in wonderful artists, trust them, and do your best to make sure everything is set up so they can work well.

2) Walk directly at the problem

Anne Bogart's book, *A Director Prepares*, is a gem if you ever feel creatively lost. When feeling scared, my impulse is often to go into myself and hide. She writes about how, when she feels stuck and doesn't know what to do, she gets up and walks directly towards the problem anyway. She chooses to act decisively despite not knowing. That physical act has helped me move through fear.

3) Know the power of a break

Know when to keep going and know when to step back and have a break. Trust that unconscious thinking will happen if you leave it alone for a bit. Thank you Sammy, I have you to thank for this.

4) Create rituals that get you through

Daisy Jacobs taught me most things I understand about the use of ritual. That word isn't as grand as it seems; I understand a ritual as having three basic principles: attention, intention and repetition. I want to listen to the rituals that the specific group of people are making anyway and amplify them. I wish that I'd leaned more into ritual to mark the big moments we passed when making *Gunter*, but feelings of stress overtook and so some moments were passed over without marking, which I think is a shame. But those smaller rituals (volleyball, throwing the ball with a name pre-show, checking-in) are all useful and grounding to return to when things get turbulent.

5) Show your work a lot

To people who love you rather than people who hate you. And know how you want them to watch it. And then really listen to what they have to say. It can be really scary and can bruise the ego, but it's the only way we found out this show had four endings (two days before we left to go to Edinburgh).

6) David Bowie: The Search is the Thing

Try to keep the energy of searching, even when you need to start pinning things down.

7) Sarah Bedi: Rules vs Freedom

Sarah Bedi, my mentor and friend, taught me most things I know about directing and leading a room. Most things come back to them. To name just one, they taught me that freedom can only come when there are rules.

8) Find connections with artists around you, not just above you

We can be tricked into thinking artistic opportunities only lie in the people ten years ahead of us, that we have to reach vertically in the hope that we will be let into some golden gates. For me, the best artistic progressions happened when I used my energy to connect horizontally, to my own peer group, to people who were at a similar career point to me.

9) Hold on tightly, let go lightly

When things are failing you, let them go. Even if you were absolutely sure it was going to work in your bedroom. (I think here of Letty Thomas and Julia Grogan playing Soggy Biscuits with absolute commitment, which I still can't believe is not in the show.)

10) To Ben

Who I told about this idea when it was just an idea, and wasn't here by the time it was a real show. You taught me to take playing very seriously, to find the silliness in everything, and to make a really, really, really big mess.

Lyds

Broadly speaking, it is difficult to access the lives of ordinary people from the past. We are guided by a cultural tradition that elevates the extraordinary, the people that are 'worth talking about', who changed the course of history, who did something with their lives. Such individuals were documented in their lifetime or perhaps they themselves could write – they are readily accessible to us and written about today. Yet this is not the case for the vast majority of people who don't appear in the traditional state archive, who weren't immortalised in art or literature, or popular print. It is here that the biases relating to gender, race, class and identity play out in the historical record and are reproduced in written histories. Whose voices have been lifted up from the past? Whose have been neglected, or consciously erased? Historians are actively challenging these archival imbalances, and it is the work of authors like Marisa J. Fuentes, Saidiya Hartman, Laura Gowing, and Natalie Zemon Davis that are the trailblazers in this movement.

Historians with an impetus to recover those voices seek to problematise and resist the limitations of traditional history and reach into the past. It is a very human urge to see how people in the past lived, what they found funny, what their stories were, how they loved, or how they expressed themselves. It is also an act of political optimism – it is our best way of making senses of ourselves and the world around us. It makes us relational, connected to a bigger picture that does far more in explaining our present context than any other tool we have. It enriches us to see the strand of connection between past and present. It can also enrage us. It is painful to confront the atrocities of how past societies acted, or the imaginative ways in which oppressive forms of bigotry break down and recover throughout the past only to emerge (or lie latent) in the present. This is the ebb and flow of history; complex, messy, and certainly not deterministic.

This is where we meet Anne Gunter. She is a rare find. Her case documents offer a unique insight into the experience of an otherwise 'ordinary' young woman from a yeoman family in a Berkshire parish from the 1600s. Without these records, which trace her story across a period of a few years before she disappears into obscurity, she would have been lost to history eternally. Her life undocumented, and therefore unreachable to us. That being said, the document is challenging to read. Her testimony is written in the sprawling hand of a court underclerk who, though highly trained, had the significant challenge of recording her verbal account; eleven pages that broke the silence of years of coercion and abuse. He no doubt modified her exact wording as he scribed. The interrogation document is clearer – these are the questions for Brian and Anne Gunter that the Star Chamber prosecution would have had time to plan. Here I want to acknowledge the late historian Jim Sharpe, whose remarkable research and patience with these documents have been essential to our work. We see in his classic account of Anne's case how instructive the record is. It tells us a huge amount about the nature of authority in the period, family relationships, patriarchy, politics, scepticism around witchcraft, and the build-up of community accusations.

It also leaves us with problems. We are confronted by the transhistorical (near universal) persistence of patriarchy and, in this particular case, how that gave rise to coercion and abuse. It is both striking and depressing that Anne's story makes sense in the world of today, over four hundred years after it happened. Then there are the practical problems. The decree outcomes for the Star Chamber cases (a court which presided over criminal and civil jurisdiction from 1485–1642) are lost. Or, as the National Archives website puts it, such records simply 'have not survived'. So, we don't know what happened to Anne after she testified against her dad. For historians, this is maddening, but for theatremakers it is an opportunity – it is the properly imaginative, interpretive part of her story. It's our licence to fill in the gaps because we aren't limited by the empirical demands of history – this is the part of making this show that I really love, and where I have learnt the most.

It has been such a gift to collaborate with so many incredible artists in reconstructing Anne's story. I have learnt so much about the value of history and good storytelling. I am totally invigorated by the way people have responded to her experience, and proud that we have managed to give her life beyond her own time.

This show is unwaveringly dedicated to Anne. We have done our best to reach her, to work with the fleeting glimpses, and to let the world know Brian Gunter was a proper bastard.

Characters

HISTORIAN
ANNE GUNTER
BRIAN GUNTER
ELIZABETH GREGORY
BRIAN GUNTER'S WIFE
NICK
PHYSICIAN
CUNNING WOMAN
MARY PEPWELL
AGNES PEPWELL
A BULL
THOMAS HINTON
JUDGE
PHILIP
JUDGE 2
ALICE
JURY
GERALD
KING JAMES
JOAN
JOAN

Note on Text

Centred text in **BOLD CAPITALS** is typed by the Historian
and appears on a projector screen.

An ellipsis (…) on its own line indicates a pause.

A dash (—) on its own line indicates either a break or a big shift
in the scene.

Note on Play

Gunter was originally performed by three actors and a historian (who also played the music).

We found the multi-roling added more life. However, we encourage you to perform it how you like.

This text went to press before the end of rehearsals and so may differ slightly from the play as performed.

Prologue

An anatomy lecture theatre.

Footage of the Ashbourne Shrovetide Football match plays on a projector screen.

A brutal medieval ball game that's still played now.

While this plays, three people come on to the stage and stand in a circle, ready to sing.

'Oh, Where the Bad Man Sleeps'

ALL.
>Oh where the bad man sleeps
>Oh Lord he's bigger than me
>Oh where the bad man sleeps
>Oh Lord he's bigger than me
>Oh where the bad man sleeps
>Oh Lord he's bigger than me
>Oh where the bad man sleeps
>Oh Lord he's bigger than me

>HISTORIAN *enters.*

HISTORIAN. Hello everyone, my name is Lydia and I'm a historian.

I'm not an actor playing a historian – it's nothing as clever as that, I'm afraid. No, I'm a historian, I read history for fun because I love it. And that means a couple of things for this show.

Firstly, I'm a bit surprised to be standing on stage at the Royal Court Theatre.

The second is that I genuinely care about history. The past is full of amazing stories that sort of just sit there unless someone bothers to tell them. And I have always believed that this story needs to be told.

Before we do that though, I wondered if I could ask you all to close your eyes for me?

That would be amazing.

…

And once they're closed, can I ask you all to picture a witch?

Just the first kind of image of a witch that comes to your mind.

…

And once you've got that you can open them –

Boo!

…

We'll come back to that later. Okay –

I wanna tell you an extraordinary story I came across a few years ago.

It's the story of Anne Gunter.

ANNE GUNTER, *a young woman, enters. She stares up at a monster above her head.*

Anne was born in 1584.

She grew up in North Moreton – a small village just outside of Oxford.

And she was nineteen when these unbelievable things started happening to her.

It goes without saying, this happened over four hundred years ago, so we've had to use our imagination a bit.

ANNE *leaves.*

But one thing we do know –

For absolute fact –

No ifs no buts no coconuts.

It all started with a game of football.

A whistle blows.

Production photographs of Julia Grogan, Hannah Jarrett-Scott and Norah Lopez Holden by Alex Brenner

THE AVERAGE ASSIZE TRIAL LASTED
FOR 20 MINUTES

THE TRIAL AGAINST ELIZABETH
LASTED FOR EIGHT HOURS

ACT ONE

Scene One

MIDSUMMER, 1604

A FOOTBALL

Mud. A football is chucked into the audience. The scene erupts into a bustling football match. 'Three Lions (Football's Coming Home)' booms over a speaker.

Two YOUNG LADS, *North Moreton boys, sprint into the space and introduce us to Shrovetide Football – a medieval football game that is physical and brutal in nature. More like wrestling. They get the crowd going. Can the ball get across the entire audience? Can we split the audience in a chant-off?*

The game is initially boyish and playful. But their innocent fun starts to tip into aggression. Something in the air shifts and the boys start scrapping. Shirt-pulling and light punches become harder as the boys start ripping at each other. Until they're caked in mud.

Behind them, BRIAN GUNTER *appears out of nowhere.*

BRIAN GUNTER, ANNE'S DAD
THE RICHEST MAN IN THE VILLAGE

He's large in stature. The wealthiest and most feared man in the village.

HISTORIAN. Now let me tell you something about Anne's dad Brian, he does not respond well to anarchy.

    BRIAN *approaches. He moves between the* LADS. *He's frightening. He pulls their heads back and in one quick motion –*

He smashes their heads together.

Blood and brains splatter across the floor.

BRIAN KILLS TWO BOYS AT A FOOTBALL MATCH

Scene Two

ELIZABETH GREGORY, *the boys' mother, is grieving. She shovels their blood and guts off the floor. As she cleans, we enter a courtroom.*

During the above action, BRIAN *gives his version of events. It's heartfelt.*

BRIAN. Look, Your Honour, let me start by saying that what happened to the Gregory boys was an absolute tragedy. But we cannot blame ourselves for it.

On the day we're talking about, the boys were playing football. They were breaking the law. Football is a game that brings out the worst in man. Violence, aggression, disrespect of local property. Something bad was bound to happen. I'm only sorry that a moment of blind hatred for the game and the threat it poses to our community, has led to the death of two North Moreton boys. For that, I am sorry.

What I won't apologise for, is my firm belief in local justice. I am a keeper of the peace. And I believe that we must root out trouble where we see it, and when there's violence, someone has to act. In this case, that person was me.

To the Gregorys –

**THEIR MUM, ELIZABETH GREGORY
DOES NOT ATTEND THE TRIAL**

ELIZABETH *stops cleaning. Lights a cig. Smoke rolls in.*

I'm sorry that your sons are no longer with us. I'm sorry that they were running reckless and out of control. I'm sorry that this had a consequence. But, Your Honour, as you've said so yourself: if football shall break the windows of houses, well, let it break the bones of those playing it.

A blues number groans. ELIZABETH *picks up a cowboy hat and sings to us.*

'Bastard Song'

ELIZABETH.
> A bastard killed my sons and has been forgiven by everyone
> A bastard split their jaw said 'Lemme hear you scream if you want some more'
> A bastard stole their life and turned me into this desperate wife
> This desperate wife cries desperately as he keeps his skin on clean and free
>
> Shoulda put poison in his dinner
> But I didn't do shit
> No I didn't do shit
>
> A bad man bashed their heads and left me in a pool of dread
> They stayed alive for a week as I listened to them softly breathe
> They said 'Forgive me, Mum, I'm not a sinner I'm a sinner's son
> Will the Lord protect our souls?' I said 'Fuck the Lord you should've grown old'
>
> Shoulda killed his babies in the night-time
> Like he did mine
> Like he did mine
>
> The system served me well. Two boys dead and an empty cell
> He's untouched and I'm in a mess, you got the wrong person but did your best
> Say no to police cuz they haven't a clue, but whilst there's still prisons they need to hold you

Thank you, Lord, nice one, state, he walks around freely but
what is my fate?

A boy band appears.

Coulda been, shoulda been – this man will drive me insane

BOY BAND.
She says she needs her babies, bad man gunna drive her crazy

ELIZABETH.
Woulda been, something in my babies losing their life

BOY BAND.
Ooh damn yeah he got them real bad, shouldn't mess with
the Gunters' dad

ELIZABETH.
You won the war
You took the coffin
But my babies didn't die for nothin, Brian Gunter

I'll make a loaf of bread and pretend my sons aren't fucking
dead
I'll play the local scold cuz I'm a woman and I'm rude and old
I'll curse your house your home and take what's mine from
the pain I hold
I'll give you some, I'll share the hurt, as I kick myself to the
fucked-up kerb

SHOULDA BEEN

COULDA BEEN

BUT I'M NOT –

BRIAN. A very good mother. That'll be all, Your Honour.

**BRIAN GUNTER WALKS FREE
FOR THE MURDER OF THE GREGORY BOYS**

Scene Three

GUNTER HOUSEHOLD

ANNE *enters, on her own. The audience meet her for a moment in her private world.*

Throughout the following the focus should be on ANNE.

BRIAN *gets home to his wife.*

WIFE. How was it, my love?

> BRIAN *puts his bag down.*

BRIAN. Parish contracts, lucky you don't have to deal with them.

WIFE. Well I'm glad you're back.

BRIAN. How's everything in the village?

WIFE. I haven't left the house. Gregory's at it again.

> BRIAN *scoffs.*

BRIAN. People need to mind their own fucking business.

Where's Annie?

WIFE. She's in her bed. It's her monthly bleed.

He goes to leave.

BRIAN. Right, I'm away out.

WIFE. What, now?

BRIAN. Nick's asked to see me.

WIFE. You've just got home.

BRIAN. And the sooner I leave, the sooner I'll return.

Door slams. ANNE *convulses again. The world shifts.*

—

THE PUB

NICK *and* BRIAN *are watching the football.*

NICK. Brian, how you getting on, mate?

BRIAN. Pull your socks up, number ten, you dozy prick.

NICK. Brian, I did actually want to talk to you –

BRIAN. Right, I haven't got long, Nick. What's this about?

NICK. Look since the whole like… murder thing… People are starting to talk.

BRIAN. I didn't come all this way to chat market gossip, Nick.

NICK. Nah it's more than that, mate. That Gregory bint ain't slowing down. Worst part is – it's catching on. People are starting to listen to her.

BRIAN *stiffens.*

BRIAN. What's she saying?

ELIZABETH. BRIAN GUNTER KILLED MY BOYS AND HE'S WALKING FREE. ARE YOU JUST GONNA SIT AND DO NOTHING? HE DOESN'T PAY HIS TAXES WHILE WE ALL STARVE AT HOME. THAT DAUGHTER ROTS IN THAT HOUSE OF HIS. LET'S BRING THE BASTARD DOWN ONCE AND FOR ALL, WE NEED TO RECLAIM POWER IN THIS VILLAGE –

DOOOOOOOOOOOOOOWN WITH GUUUUNTER –

BRIAN *is visibly angry. Gains composure.*

BRIAN. She said what?

BRIAN*'s face hardens.*

I've got to get home.

BRIAN *leaves. He arrives home reading a pamphlet. He pours a drink, wakes* ANNE *up and gives it to her. She drinks.*

—

GUNTER HOUSEHOLD

BRIAN *remains staring at* ANNE *throughout this scene, as if his wife isn't there.*

BRIAN. She's sick. I've sent for a physician.

WIFE. She's fine. It's just her monthly bleed.

BRIAN. Well it's clearly not, is it.

WIFE. It'll pass. She's like it every time.

BRIAN. No, she's not right. I know my Annie. I want her looked at now.

WIFE. Brian, we can't just –

BRIAN (*snaps*). Don't tell me what I can and can't do in my own fucking house.

She stares at him fearfully. He softens.

Look, I can see you're scared. I'm scared too. We need to hold our nerve.

—

ANNE drinks the rest of the drink, BRIAN *watches. Blackout.* ANNE *sings.*

ANNE.
Where did the birds go now? Where's their call?
I can't hear them. I can't hear them. Were they here at all?

—

GUNTER HOUSEHOLD

PHYSICIAN. Where is she?

BRIAN. She's fitted twice within the hour.

PHYSICIAN. It stinks.

BRIAN. We closed the windows to keep the humours in.

PHYSICIAN. The youth have great strength to withstand disease, Brian. Are the convulsions violent?

BRIAN. Like the wrath of God drumming her body.

PHYSICIAN walks into ANNE*'s eyeline.*

PHYSICIAN. She needs a decent purging. Free her from any deadly disease.

ANNE *raises her arm slowly. Blood trickles down the length of it. It is black.*

I'll return in two days. God be with you.

—

HALLUCINATION. Suddenly the world turns upside down. ANNE *sings.*

ANNE.
Oh my daddy said to me
If a woman lives in halves you're half the woman you
   should be
I'm a dog when I am sick

PHYSICIAN *howls.*

Barking for the stick
Here they take penance for my soul

—

GUNTER HOUSEHOLD

PHYSICIAN. Brian, are you aware of anyone in the village who might want to cause your daughter harm?

BRIAN *considers...*

BRIAN. There is a woman who holds our family in contempt, but it's market gossip.

PHYSICIAN. I've been observing Anne for four days now. And whatever this is, it's beyond natural remedy.

I think it's time to call on the cunning folk.

—

ANNE (*singing*).
Here they take penance for my soul
Hear it sudden driftwood sudden driftwood take me home –

—

GUNTER HOUSEHOLD

Whip crack. A leather-clad CUNNING WOMAN *stands before* BRIAN.

CUNNING WOMAN. Alright, Old Gunter, get your cock out, you little shitty pig.

Beat.

BRIAN. That's not why I called.

Whip drops.

CUNNING WOMAN (*genuine concern*). What is it?

BRIAN. My Anne is sick. You're the only person in the village who can determine whether the causes are unnatural. Please help us.

She kneels before ANNE, *maternal.*

CUNNING WOMAN. Bubby, I am so sorry. Daddy asked me to cum quickly and we had a little confusion.

Let's see what's at play.

She stares at the back of ANNE*'s head.*

Annie.

ANNE *doesn't respond at all to any of the following.*

Round we come, bubby.

Round we come.

Come on, Annie.

Turn and face.

Round we come.

Round we come. Round we come. Round we come. Round we come.

Round we come. Round we come.

Come on, Annie.

Round we come.

Round we come.

Round we –

ANNE *erupts into squeals.* CUNNING WOMAN *jumps, she looks to* BRIAN. *She's fearful.*

Okay, let's try…

She hums, crawling over to ANNE. *And lays her head on her back. She senses motion. She lies like this for quite some time, before concluding…*

Okay. Yes. He's here. Satan is here.

He's lap-dancing. He's fetching away her soul.

She rises, carrying the weight of the world on her shoulders.

Brian, your daughter's been bewitched –

HISTORIAN *interjects –*

HISTORIAN. To be clear: there is a difference between a witch and someone who is being bewitched, or possessed.

A witch is defined as someone who causes harm using dark magic, whilst to be possessed is to have a demonic spirit enter your body.

So in the seventeenth century, the witch is the criminal perpetrator, and the possessed is the victim of her harm.

The CUNNING WOMAN *hastily leaves.*

BRIAN (*almost to self*). It wants revenge. My poor girl. My beautiful girl.

ANNE *squeals, terrified; she tries to make herself into the smallest ball possible.*

Did you hear that, Annie?

Who would…

Help us.

We need help.

ANNE *begins to whisper.*

What?

ANNE *whispers.* BRIAN *turns to her.*

Yes, yes, yes, Anne, what did you say? Who did this to you, Anne?

ANNE *stutters.*

Use your words, my love. Try your hardest. Go on, Anne, speak. What is it, my girl? –

ANNE *looks like she's going to vomit, oh God she really is going to... She starts to cough like a cat. She coughs up a very long blonde hair, she pulls it out of her throat and thrusts it into the light.*

Gregory.

HISTORIAN *interjects again –*

HISTORIAN. In this case, Elizabeth was the witch, and Anne the victim.

BRIAN *breaks out to the villagers.*

BRIAN. Gregory

GREGORY

GREGORY

He begins to get the villagers going until everyone is chanting 'Gregory' –

GREGORY

GREGORY

GREGORY

GREGORY

He is wild with it now, like an animal.

GREGORY

GREGORY

GREGORY

ANNE *doesn't move her mouth, but a dark groaning voice erupts from nowhere –*

VOICE. ELIZABETH GREGORY IN COVENANT WITH THE DEVIL HAS VISITED ME TO TAKE MY SOUL WITH HER FAMILIAR THE BEAR.

Silence.

HISTORIAN. And finally, every witch would be identified with a familiar. An animal that represented the Devil that would never leave their side. The black cat. Or in this case –

BRIAN (*into mic*). It's Elizabeth Gregory and the bear!!!

SHOW LIGHTS!!!!!!!!!!!!!!!!

ANNE NAMES ELIZABETH GREGORY AS A WITCH

The world is the wrong way up, again. We enter another hallucination. A woman and a bear, or a woman as a bear, or a bear eating a woman. But make it cabaret.

'Honey' by Robyn plays.

MAKE IT ANYTHING.

Sexy

Scary

Beautiful

Sad

Unfair

Animalistic

Girly –

HISTORIAN. Anne names two other women, a local mother and daughter who already have a reputation as suspected witches. Their names were –

We come back to ANNE*'s bedroom. She doesn't move her mouth, but a dark groaning voice erupts again –*

BRIAN (*into mic*). MARY PEPWELL. WITH THE SWAN!

Spotlight on MARY. *She is out of this world. All dressed in black and covered in feathers. She wears pointe shoes. Think: Black Swan on crack.*

We come back to ANNE*'s bedroom. And again, the voice from nowhere:*

VOICE. AGNES PEPWELL WITH THE BUULLLLLLLLLL!!

A BULL *enters the stage. One description could be: a spotlight falls on a* BULL *who is just SICK of being poked and prodded, it enters the bullring sad and tired.*

We watch – for an uncomfortable amount of time – the BULL *try to resurrect its sorry ass from the soil and perform. Do the audience throw things at it?*

Through the chaos, an exhausted and scared ELIZABETH *sings to us.*

'Bad Man Reprise'

ELIZABETH.
Oh when he comes for me
That man got news for me
Oh when he takes me down
Bad man he breaks me down
Oh when he looks at me
He puts his hooks me

Said oh when he takes me down
The bad man sleeps…

Simultaneously, ANNE *goes to a Bible and takes an oath.*

The text (though you cannot hear it) goes something like this…

BRIAN *first,* ANNE *repeats:*

'Never to disclose any of those things –

Never to disclose any of those things –

Which I have sworn to keep secret –

Which I have sworn to keep secret – '

HISTORIAN. There are many ways to test a witchcraft accusation.

In this story the villagers stripped Elizabeth Gregory naked and burnt her hair.

The theory was that if you burnt the witch's hair and the possessed victim stopped fitting it would prove a connection between the two.

ELIZABETH.
I don't know where the bad man sleeps…

A blood-curdling scream. ELIZABETH *is dragged from the circle. Her hair is pulled out and set alight. It burns bright and fast.*

ANNE *stops fitting.* BRIAN *delights in this.*

HISTORIAN. The villagers believe that Elizabeth is a witch. And a court date is set.

IF FOUND GUILTY,
THE WOMEN WILL HANG

Music starts, BRIAN *and* ANNE *come together.*

BRIAN TAKES ANNE TO OXFORD UNIVERSITY
IN ORDER TO PROVE POSSESSION

This remains on screen during next chunk.

ACT TWO

Scene One

TO PROVE POSSESSION

BRIAN *is presenting* ANNE*'s bewitchment to the academics at Oxford University. It is a plea/call-to-arms, and he is nervous about it.*

BRIAN. Hello. Evening. Afternoon.

Coughs.

OXFORD UNIVERSITY, AUG 1605

Um, it was a surprisingly long journey here.

…

My name is Brian.

I am grateful to the staff, who organised the food. And the journey.

Thank you, Robert and Brian. Brian.

Um.

Cough.

I'm not used to this

format

of things, my field of work is, well, exactly that – in the field. Head in the grass not the books.

But I'm sure we can come together with this common purpose: to prosecute those who are causing deep pain.

I am taking Elizabeth Gregory and her accomplices to court. The trial will be held in Abingdon in thirty days.

My daughter is being bewitched. And I need you all to see that.

And to say that you've seen that to get the justice we deserve.

If you will, please, testify to save my daughter.

Beat.

I invite you now to watch the unnatural becoming of a girl possessed.

ANNE *comes through the curtain. She stands there, uncertain. And then something takes over her.*

ANNE'S PERFORMANCE

ANNE *performs before a room of Oxford academics.*

Our song reference: 'I Can Never Go Home Anymore' by The Shangri-Las.

ANNE.
I got home early one night
Fixed myself a drink
There he was in the cold blue light
I didn't know what to think

I can't remember clearly what happened next
I suppose I lit a cigarette
Those were the moments of calm
As I watched my life undress

I am not a victim
I'm a addicted to this victim of mine
You've got a seven-inch gun in your hand honey
What are you gonna do?
Why?

'Cause you can never go home any more
You can never, go home any mo–

I contemplate pulling the trigger against his fine temple
But then I think of what a mess it will make
So I think of something less bloody

Like asking for all the money he owes me so we can all get
    on with our shitty little lives
So did you do it?
Yeah, I settled on his stomach
The place he like to eat
Symbolic don't you think? All that booze and all that meat
All that liquor all that wine
The sweat that stains my sheets
What did you do to him honey
That's a think I can't repeat

I cleaned him with a cloth of his favourite colour blue
Like the lace I used to wear when I started loving you
Do you remember how we used to laugh in summer nights
    in June?
Well Daddy you bastard
Daddy we're through

You can never, go home any more
You can never, go home anymo–

I don't remember the nights
I don't remember what I was wearing
I don't remember the traffic lights running red
Or if I was caring
I don't remember anything
It's like God have I got amnesia or something?

You can never go home any more
You can never go home any more

According to the archives, ANNE *demonstrated the
following:*

Contortion and flexibility

Violent convulsions

Abnormal swelling

Muscular contortions

Rigidity of the limbs

Preternatural strength

Vomiting pins

Turning backwards on her hands

Going upon her ankles in a 'strange and stiff manner'

Conversing in languages of which she had no previous knowledge

Speaking in a deep beastly voice that differed from her normal voice

Contempt for sacred objects

Uttered blasphemies

Went into trances

Foresaw the future

Body became heavier

Her clothing would move – her garters would unravel and the bodice of her petticoat would unlace

Collective crying

...

GOOD LUCK.

Scene Two

BRIAN *clears up after the performance. He removes the feathers and honey and wigs and trainers from the stage. Meanwhile the actor playing* ANNE *is cleaned up.*

Then BRIAN *sits down and destroys a pie.*

As the HISTORIAN *speaks, the following counts down on the board:*

9 DAYS UNTIL THE TRIAL AGAINST ELIZABETH, MARY + AGNES

8 DAYS UNTIL THE TRIAL AGAINST ELIZABETH, MARY + AGNES

7 DAYS UNTIL THE TRIAL AGAINST ELIZABETH, MARY + AGNES

6 DAYS UNTIL THE TRIAL AGAINST ELIZABETH, MARY + AGNES

5 DAYS UNTIL THE TRIAL AGAINST ELIZABETH, MARY + AGNES

HISTORIAN. My role as I understand it is to guide the reconstruction of Anne's story by rooting it in its history. That role becomes difficult when dealing with the private, more speculative aspects of her story. The parts that weren't written down, or if they were, were written in a very particular way by a particular voice.

To put it plainly, there is an inherent eroticism to the spectacle of Anne's possession, and a sexualisation of her in the accounts from her observers. Men were obsessed with her body and clothes. They talked about her clothes mysteriously unlacing themselves, or her body weight becoming inexplicably heavier. They would marvel at her body as a site of supernatural activity. Though these accounts are always written in veiled language – as an examination or an assessment, the sexuality is implied but never stated explicitly.

So I am left to imagine what was happening to her in the rooms where she was kept. And what I am imagine unsettles me.

Because whatever it was, it was compelling enough to convince every man who witnessed her in Oxford to testify in court. Every single one until –

Enter THOMAS HINTON –

THOMAS. Mind if I come in?

BRIAN *looks up from his pie, shocked and unprepared.*

BRIAN. Thomas Hinton! It's an honour to have you on the case. Your testimony on this will be the nail in the coffin. If you'll pardon the pun.

Fancy a drink?

THOMAS. I'm actually here to have a little word with Anne, if that's okay.

BRIAN. Let's me and you have a drink first and then we'll get her in.

THOMAS. I was hoping to see her in private.

Beat.

BRIAN. Why do you want to do that?

THOMAS. Matter of protocol with these things.

BRIAN. You of all people know how exhausting this whole thing has been. She's asleep.

THOMAS. Really, I must insist.

BRIAN. What are you wanting alone time with my little girl for, Thomas?

Beat.

THOMAS. I need to see that the Devil is at work.

BRIAN. You saw him at work only yesterday.

THOMAS. I need to see it closer up –

BRIAN. You saw the way her garters unlaced without anyone touching them. Did you stay for the levitation?

THOMAS. Yes, but I know that the eye can trick and I know from experience how crucial a valuable witness can be in a case like yours.

THOMAS *tries to push past* BRIAN.

BRIAN. Jesus, Thomas, I've just said, the girl's sleeping. She's not prepared for visitors.

THOMAS. If you want me to testify. I can't have any doubt.

BRIAN *stiffens, his heart rate flies up to 110%.*

BRIAN. Right.

...

Well as I said –

...

ANNE!

...

I think she's in her –

ANNE, COME HERE –

ANNE *slowly emerges in a night robe, she looks knackered. Her eyes hollow, her body tired.*

THOMAS. Hello Anne, my name is Thomas Hinton. I am here because I'm going to be called upon to testify in the court case. I will be asked to confirm that your possession has been brought about by Elizabeth Gregory.

That she's a witch.

Beat.

Do you know where she is right now, Anne?

ANNE *looks at him.*

They've had to keep her in a holding cell, because the village turned so violent towards her.

BRIAN *looks smug.*

So, in order to testify with good conscience, I'm going to need something from you.

I need you to show me a trick.

Or something.

Someone says you can fly?

Nothing. ANNE *doesn't know what to do.*

How about…

He starts writing a word on a piece of paper.

HISTORIAN. One of Anne's recorded tricks was her second sight. Someone would write a random word on a piece of paper, hide it, and Anne could tell them what it said. The word could be anything, such as –

THOMAS. What's the word, Anne?

HISTORIAN. 'Sausages', for example.

THOMAS. Okay well done, very impressive, let's try again.

HISTORIAN. Or 'rabbit', maybe.

THOMAS. Now that's just showing off. Okay I'm going to try one last time, but –

HISTORIAN. This time, Thomas Hinton tried something else…

THOMAS. Do you mind if I blow out the candles?

HISTORIAN *turns to our Deputy Stage Manager.*

HISTORIAN. Aime, can we turn the lights out please?

Darkness. Silence. Scratch of pencil on paper.

Long pause.

THOMAS. Anne? What's the word, Anne? Anne?

Boom. Lights back up. BRIAN *is trying to take off* ANNE*'s gown for* THOMAS*'s pleasure.* THOMAS*, appalled, pulls away from* BRIAN.

I'll see you in court, Brian.

4 DAYS UNTIL THE TRIAL AGAINST
ELIZABETH, MARY + AGNES

BOOM.

THOMAS *takes the mic.*

He writes a letter to his good friend and overall trusty nice guy, Judge David Williamson, who will run the case against Elizabeth Gregory.

A big tune plays underscoring it. Something like 'I Was Gonna Fight Fascism' by Alabaster dePlume.

THOMAS (*into mic*). Dear Judge David,

How are the kids?

It has come to my attention that the much-discussed Anne Gunter, due to attend your court proceedings next week, is a charlatan and a fraud. North Moreton has been hoodwinked, bamboozled, and led astray. Her appearance of bewitchment is simply a display of trickery. It is the work of human earthly malice, and not of the Devil as she would have you believe. In other words

GUNTER IS A FUCKING LIAR.

Kisses,

Hinton.

Scene Three

ABINGDON ASSIZE COURT

THE WITCH TRIAL AGAINST
ELIZABETH, MARY + AGNES

MARY, AGNES *and* ELIZABETH *sing together. A final song before they receive their fate. They each hold the masks of the bear, swan and the bull.*

'Scupper the Man'

MARY/AGNES/ELIZABETH.
    Lord scupper the man for once
    Take him for what he's worth
    Swear on the heart of a baby
    He's the one that caused the hurt
    Take him for what he wants
    I'm the one that fed the earth
    Fed the earth

    Lord scupper the man for once
    Give him the blood he knows
    Swear on the heart of a baby
    He's the one that tore the fold
    Take him what he wants
    I'm the one that bled in birth
    Fed the earth
    Take him for what he wants
    I'm the one that bled in birth
    Fed the earth.

THE AVERAGE ASSIZE TRIAL
LASTED FOR 20 MINUTES

ANNE'S CASE LASTED FOR EIGHT HOURS

The rhythm of the new music drops in – MARY *and* AGNES *drop away leaving* ELIZABETH *front and centre.*

The following song is rhythmic and spoken.

'Court Song'

JUDGE.

I think it's time to hear from another one
Have we got a Philip in attendance, Johnson's son?

PHILIP.

Yes I'm here and I have my truth to be told
Elizabeth Gregory's a witch and a scold!

JUDGE.

If you'd like to go from the start, Philip, perhaps it would be
good to tell the jury when you first noticed a change in
Elizabeth? If you could do it within an eight-bar rhythm too
that would be great.

PHILIP.

Well, I noticed in mass in the saying of the peace
That Elizabeth Gregory would start to sneeze

ELIZABETH.

I HAD A COLD

PHILIP.

She SHOUTS when she has something to say
On the occasion in question she refused to pray

JUDGE.

Are you claiming, Philip, that Elizabeth is working against
Christ?

PHILIP.

Well, she's certainly not working with him

JUDGE.

Interesting. Next to the stand

JUDGE 2.

Alice Kirfoote, Brian Gunter's neighbour

ALICE.

I saw, what I saw
Elizabeth Gregory's an eyesore

JUDGE.

That's inadmissible evidence. Not fact

ALICE.
Fine, well she should go and shave her back

JUDGE.
Alice, this is serious – life or death – the jury needs to hear
EXACTLY what you've seen

ALICE.
Well her and her husband don't share the same bed and
haven't done it for years if you know what I mean…

ELIZABETH.
I'm a bad woman
But you ain't seen nothing yet

PEOPLE.
Elizabeth Gregory has sold her soul to the Devil, did you
know never does as she's told

JURY.
She's a bad woman
Think she's done something that she'll regret

JUDGE.
Next to the stand
Nicholas Kirfoote, friend of Brian Gunter. You're here to do
a character testimony

NICK.
Yep. He's a niiiiiiiiiiiiiice guy. He's a friendly guy. He's
always bringing round bits and stuff. You know, he's a nice
guy. But that's actually beside the point because what
I actually want to say is that she's a baaaaaaaaaaaad woman

ALL.
I think she's done something that she'll regret

PEOPLE.
Elizabeth Gregory has got split ends, she's a fugly slut and
she's got no friends

JURY.
She's a bad woman
Think she's done something that she'll regret

JUDGE.

Next to the stand is Gerald Duckit, claims Elizabeth Gregory told you to –

GERALD.

Pick up my litter which I thought was ironic considering she caused a plague and that plague was bubonic – and that plague killed my wife not before my three kids and the cheek of Gregory asking me for two quid at the market a week after I'd laid them all to rest, and I saw it in her eyes before I felt it in my chest that she caused all this ill and all the pain in the world and it's no coincidence that the Devil likes old girls, and so he trapped her in his snare and she gladly took the bait, they dine unholy Sabbaths where Satan bakes the cake, and they agree their evil mission to make people fucking SAD so believe me when I tell you that this WOMAN IS MAD AND SHE'S BAD AND SHE'S GLAD THAT I'M NO LONGER A DAD IN THIS STUPID LITTLE VILLAGE THAT WAS ALL THAT I HAD SO SHE HAS TO BE A WITCH AND IT ISN'T JUST A FAD IT IS GOD'S HONEST TRUTH SHE IS BAD SHE IS BAD SHE IS BAD SHE IS BAD BAD SHE'S A BAD

ANNE *tries to make a run for it. Song ends.*

BRIAN. See! She fits!

ANNE *stops moving.* BRIAN *turns out to the jury.*

Anne is a true child of God. She is kind, gentle-natured and forgiving. She makes me a better person. She makes me live honourably. When she was born, the first time she cried I saw the colour of her soul and it was golden. And, Your Honour and men of the jury, this brutal animal of Satan has stained it.

He turns to ELIZABETH.

Elizabeth Gregory, the sight of you appals me. The smell of you sickens me. You have dragged my daughter to Hell and you deserve to be punished for it.

(To the jury.) People of the jury, I say to you: I am an honest man. I wouldnae say boo to a goose! Do you honestly

believe I would put us through all of this to damage a woman's reputation? If you do, you have me wrong. If you don't, we need to work together to do away with this human plague from our community.

Beat.

Right let's finish this once and for all. Here is something that the jury cannot dispute. A spell. This spell, if read by the witch, will provoke an unnatural response in the victim, in the bewitched. Your Honour, I request that Elizabeth reads this spell.

He nods to ANNE *who moves forwards towards* ELIZABETH. ANNE, *as instructed, picks up the bear mask and thrusts it at* ELIZABETH.

ELIZABETH *reluctantly takes it.* ANNE *walks to the other side of the room and prepares for the spell. She breathes deeply. Behind her,* ELIZABETH *slowly puts on the bear mask.*

ANNE, *now ready, bounces on the balls of her feet. She turns and –*

She sees ELIZABETH. *Who's now small and scared. Her body pressed against the cell for protection.* ANNE *softens. She moves towards her.*

ELIZABETH *eventually takes off the bear mask. She stares into* ANNE*'s eyes.*

Something has moved ANNE. *But not moved her to fly. Or perform a magic trick.*

The women look at each other. Properly. For the first time.

BRIAN *stares at his daughter, his eyes burning the back of her head, willing her to do something.*

He swallows a smile.

BRIAN. Anne, I can see you're in a great deal of distress, aren't you, love. Let's take five. Have a drink –

He moves towards ANNE *to offer her water, just as she's about to sip –*

HISTORIAN. What does the name Thomas Hinton mean to you, Brian?

BRIAN *stops moving, stunned at the arrival of the* HISTORIAN.

BRIAN. He's the MP for Wiltshire.

The HISTORIAN *remains non-judgemental, impartial to the events. Like she's just opened her textbook and has one time only to ask* BRIAN *the questions.*

HISTORIAN. When did you last see him?

BRIAN. He stopped by briefly in the evening. He saw Anne perform an erotic trick.

Beat.

HISTORIAN. Judge David Williamson received a letter from Thomas Hinton on the 14th May, 1605.

Three days after he called in to see Anne.

BRIAN *shifts, knocked off-centre.*

BRIAN. What does it say?

HISTORIAN. He said Brian Gunter is a fucking liar.

BRIAN *half-laughs. It should feel awkward. Like the actor's forgotten lines. The more awkward, the better.*

HISTORIAN *closes her textbook.*

Then BRIAN *turns out to the audience. He pulls a pamphlet out of his pocket and our play continues –*

BRIAN. No, no, no, no, when Alice Samuel was executed for bewitchment she read a spell and the victim was SPINNING ON THE FUCKING CEILING and they BELIEVED her and she was HANGED FOR IT. They hanged HER ENTIRE FAMILY FOR IT. Her HUSBAND. Her EIGHT-YEAR-OLD

DAUGHTER. DEAD. So READ the SPELL AGAIN. It will work. IT HAS TO WORK. STUPID. STUPID. STUPID.

**ELIZABETH, MARY + AGNES
ARE FOUND NOT GUILTY**

The women walk out, leaving BRIAN.

ACT THREE

Scene One

Everything is falling apart for BRIAN. *A man dissolving/ combusting in front of our very eyes. The actor will essentially morph into* KING JAMES I. *Who is Scottish.*

BRIAN. Stupid fffffffffffffffffffffffffffffffffffffffffffffffff

They've made a mockery – Mockery

My daughter has been bewitched.

…

Has she?

My daughter has been bewitched.

…

Has she?

Pins

You fucking –

…

Anne, we're going to see the King.

I'm taking you to see the. To prove. To –

…

To get this to the highest place possible.

…

We're going to the King. So he can see

We need the King to see that you've been

Burps.

That you've been bewitch–

…

Your Majesty, Your Majesty, I'm sure our case has not gone under your radar but you see I am fearful.

Fearful.

Fearful.

Fearful…

…

Fearful…

The fearful abundance at this time and in this country is the detestable agent of the Devil.

JAMES I

NO, JAMES, NO WE DON'T SAY THAT ANY MORE
THE POLITICIANS DON'T –

HE IS KNOWN AS A WITCHCRAFT FANATIC

But I know how to find them, and I know how to kill them it's proven in the Scripture I can feel it in my blood –

We can't kill them any more that was before you came to England you're different noooooooow – you're safe – you're safe now

HE HAS OVERSEEN THE DEATH
OF OVER 300 WOMEN IN SCOTLAND

James, you've seen it with your own eyes a lawful medical practice it's clear as day your Christian duty thou shall not kill, James

Thou shall not kill

You must remember that

Thou shall not

Thou shall not

Thou shall not

Thou shall

Thou

James…

ANNE *creeps up behind, hiding in the shadows. He can sense her there. He sniffs. He's shocked, like she's a celeb and he's a fan. He goes to speak…*

KING JAMES. So you've been possessed.

Silence. ANNE *remains hidden behind him.*

Not speaking, hm? Yes, I wrote about that in my book, you see. It's often the case. The bewitched unable to speak.

Silence. Eyes childlike.

What's it like?

Smacks himself.

No, James.

You have to understand, Anne –

I'm under a lot of pressure to.

Believe that in this case, you haven't been… bewitched.

There's talk here at the castle, you see. It's not – it wouldn't be good. It wouldn't be a good thing to hang the – It's not done as much now. Witches. As much as I'd –

He shakes himself again.

So you have to understand my predicament.

During your stay you'll be assessed by my physicians, sceptics and the Archbishop of Canterbury. The following weeks will be thorough and potentially uncomfortable. But you must understand that in order to give a firm conclusion I need to be entirely sure. I need to believe you.

If I don't, you and your father will go on trial for fraud.

Something passes ANNE*'s stoic face, she starts to panic.*

But if I do…

Sparkle in his eyes.

Well the three – (*Excited satanic voice.*) witche– women will be hanged and you'll walk free.

So, make yourself and home. I hope I can trust you. Oh and enjoy the palace.

ANNE *is left alone. She paces, desperately panicked.*

She picks up a pin, tries to swallow it. Gags. Tries again. Gags. She gets scared. She stands there, darkness closing in. She's alone. She takes a fistful of pins and swallows them. And more. And more. We stay with her for a while, before –

Scene Two

JOAN *and* JOAN *are sitting at opposite ends of a long table. Applying Halloween make-up.*

MAIDSERVANTS AT THE PALACE
TAKE THE NIGHT OFF

THEY ARE CALLED JOAN

AND JOAN

JOAN. I mean the poor thing.

JOAN. Honestly it's hard to watch.

JOAN. Litany of abuse. For days and days and days. It's been relentless.

JOAN. Relentless.

JOAN. I'm exhausted even watching it.

JOAN. Me too.

JOAN. I mean, I don't know how a person rebuilds after this. Your sense of self just… poof out the window. Until you're left a floppy lonely mess on the floor, wondering what happened. Why everyone's out to get you.

What a poor poor poor poor poor…

Man.

Beat.

Honestly, the second I laid eyes on Brian I wanted to give him a big hug. So misunderstood.

JOAN. So misunderstood.

JOAN. And the pile-on. The scepticism. Meanwhile Elizabeth Gregory's swanning around freely having possessed a poor man's child. Honestly, a woman claims victimhood these days and they all gaggle round like gannets. Nipping and gnawing.

JOAN. It's a headache.

JOAN. Trauma this and trauma that. Back in my day you were *lucky* to get male attention. It was welcomed. Didn't get anywhere if you weren't sexually desired.

JOAN. Absolutely.

JOAN. Well of course you'd know all about that, Joan.

JOAN *nods in agreement.*

Bloody Elizabeth.

They've got a name for everything these days, I tell you.

JOAN. Attention-seekers.

JOAN. Political correctness gone mad, Joan.

JOAN. Well we'll see what happens, eh, if they're taken to court or not. What if they're found guilty for lying?

JOAN. Oh it's all pathetic, absolutely pathetic. If that man goes behind bars for this, well I've lost faith in it all.

Hush hush.

JOAN. You just want to have a little snog with him, don't you, Joan.

JOAN. Oh stop it, you cheeky beggar –

JOAN. Oooh, Gunter, look at my tits –

Oooh, Gunter, look at my fits –

She imitates fitting.

JOAN. Oooh Gunter I've been bewitched –

ANNE *CRACKS.*

FROM THE BOTTOM OF HER BELLY SHE BEGINS TO SING.

'Bad Man Sleeps Reprise'

ANNE.
I know where the bad man sleeps
I know where the bad man sleeps
He's bigger than me
Oh Lord he's bigger than me
I know where the bad man sleeps
I know where the bad man sleeps
He's bigger than me
Oh Lord he's bigger than me

ANNE *repeats this over and over and over again –*

The music evolves, the rhythm quickens and parts of ANNE *begin to loosen bit by bit. Imagine the lie slowly being released from each part of her body – freeing her. This might look like a dance.*

Whatever it is – make it euphoric and beautiful.

Enter BRIAN –

BRIAN. Annie, did you catch that?

ANNE *stops in her tracks.*

They don't believe us.

…

We're going on trial, Anne.

Do you know what that means?

…

Now it's very important we stick together.

We're a team, I want you to remember that.

We will practise what we're going to say. And they will believe us. And it will be okay.

When we go to court we will tell them the truth.

The truth is you've been bewitched, haven't you, Annie?

We aren't liars. Are we?

So we will say that when we stand up.

He places his forehead against hers.

ANNE *stares blankly at him and nods.*

…

I love you so much.

It will be okay, Annie.

BRIAN *leaves.* ANNE *cries and cries and cries and cries.*

Scene Three

STAR CHAMBER, FEB 1606

THE TRIAL AGAINST BRIAN AND ANNE

Stars dot the ceiling. ANNE *takes to the stand. She stands in
the middle of the space for what feels like an eternity. She stares
at the microphone in front of her.*

ANNE. It started with a…

…

It all started with a…

…

It all started with a game of football –

FIREWORK

ANNE *blinks up at the firework. Confused. She doesn't know
whether to carry on.*

…

I was never bew–

FIREWORK

*Where the hell – ? Bright lights erupt. Starting to get faster.
Starting to combine into a display.*

My father made m–

*She starts getting drowned out. She starts to cry. What the
hell is happening?*

She looks at BRIAN. *She goes up to him.*

I see you now. I see you. You FUCKING MONSTER.

I SEE YOU NOW.

He doesn't even flinch, he just leaves.

She considers. Right. She runs up to the HISTORIAN *and with pleading eyes –*

What happened to her?

Do I die now? Does she die? What does it say?

HISTORIAN *stares back at her blankly.*

…

DOES HE DIE?

HISTORIAN *shakes her head.*

OF COURSE NOT. THEY NEVER DO.

She's really shouting over the fireworks now.

What do I do then?

Do I just carry on then?

I can't just carry on!

FIREWORK
FIREWORK FIREWORK FIREWORK

FIREWORK

**ANNE'S TRIAL WAS DELAYED BECAUSE
GUNPOWDER WAS FOUND UNDER PARLIAMENT**

**THE OUTCOME IS UNKNOWN
THE RECORDS WERE LOST**

IT GOT LOST

IN ALL THE CHAOS

WE FORGOT

ANNE *tries to destroy the projection, but she can't. Because it's a projection.*

She shows us how she did the pin-swallowing trick.

See, it was in my finger.

It was in my FUCKING FINGER!

'Bad Man Sleep Reprise'

Oh where the bad man sleeps
Oh Lord he's bigger than me
Oh Lord he's bigger than me
Oh where the bad man sleeps
Oh Lord he's bigger than me
Oh Lord he's bigger than me

The music drops out and it's just singing –

**TAX RECORDS SHOW THAT BRIAN GUNTER
CONTINUED TO BE THE RICHEST MOST
POWERFUL MAN IN THE VILLAGE,
UNSCATHED BY THE WHOLE THING**

ANNE *sees this on the board. She goes over to the laptop and yanks out the cable. The screen fizzes to black.*

FIREWORK

FIREWORK

FIREWORK

FIREWORK
FIREWORK
FIREWORK

HISTORIAN *enters.*

HISTORIAN. You know that witch that I asked you to picture at the start of this show, let's imagine her again. Close your eyes if you want. Got her? And now I want you to imagine yourself going up to her, taking off her pointy hat, putting her broomstick in the bin and giving the black cat to a trusty neighbour.

Because there are no witches in this story. There was never a bewitchment. It was an imagination, a fantasy, a lie.

A lie that was allowed to happen.

We have no idea what happened to Anne Gunter, or the outcome of the trial. The final decree for that Star Chamber case is lost to history, and beyond that there is no sure record of what happened to her. No death certificate in the North Moreton parish where her family was buried, where Brian himself would be laid to rest in 1628; she isn't even recorded in the family will, there's nothing. Anne appeared fleetingly in the vast movement of history – until she was of no further interest to those who had the power to record it.

But there is an image that brings me comfort. The last thing we know for sure about Anne, is that after testifying against her dad for coercing, drugging, and exploiting her, she would have travelled down the Thames on a boat at dusk from the Star Chamber Court. I like to think she had the wind in her hair and a fag in her hand.

ANNE *turns out to the audience. She lights a sparkler. When the sparkler finishes, the show ends.*

Oh, Where The Bad Man Sleeps

From 'Gunter'

Composed by Lydia Higman
Orchestrated by Tom Alford

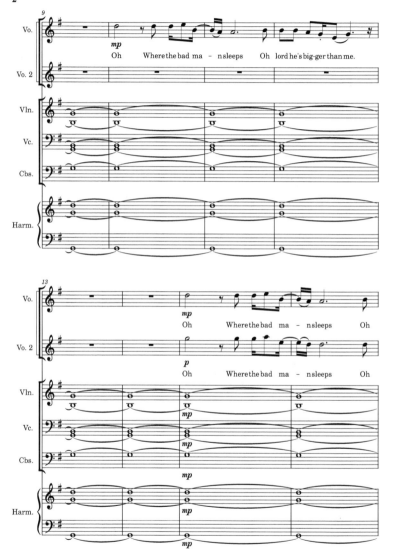

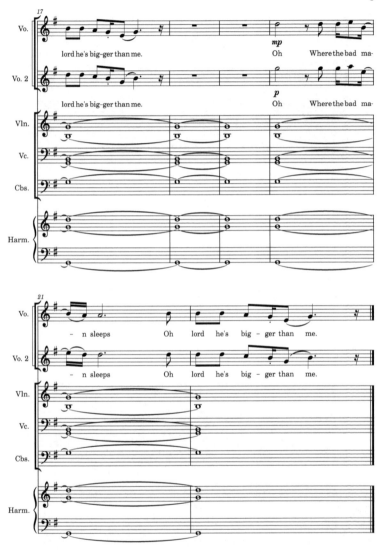

A Nick Hern Book

Gunter first published in Great Britain in 2024 as a paperback original by Nick Hern Books Limited, The Glasshouse, 49 Goldhawk Road, London W12 8QP, in association with Dirty Hare

Cover image: Doug Higman

Designed and typeset by Nick Hern Books, London
Printed in the UK by Mimeo Ltd, Huntingdon, Cambridgeshire PE29 6XX

A CIP catalogue record for this book is available from the British Library

ISBN 978 1 83904 338 3

www.nickhernbooks.co.uk/environmental-policy